A Book About My Grandparents

A Child's Creation

Randi Lynn Millward

Instructions:

This book is a children's activity book. The sentences are started but left incomplete for the child to finish in his or her own words. The adjacent pages are intentionally blank so that the child may create his or her own illustrations.

The artist may draw with crayons or colored pencils, tape pictures to the pages, use stickers, or us any other parent-approved age-appropriate artistic medium that doesn't seep through the paper.

ISBN-13: 978-1-943771-09-7
ISBN-10: 1-943771-09-X

More books by this author may be found at www.Amazon.com and other participating retailers.

A Book About My Grandparents

by

____

Age: ______________

Date: _____________

My grandparents are

____

____

____

____

____

____________________.

My grandparents live

____

____

____

____

____

____________________.

My grandparents like to

____

____

____

____

____

___________________.

My grandparents don't like

____

____

____

____

____

____________________.

My grandparents are really good at

____

____

____

____

__________________.

I like when my grandparents

____

____

____

____

____

____

____

____________________________.

My grandparents like when I

____

____

____

____

____

____

____________________________.

My favorite thing to do with my grandparents is

____

____

____

____

___________________.

I have fun when my grandparents and I

____

____

____

____

____

_____________________.

My grandparents say

____

____

____

____

____

____

____________________________.

I like to show my grandparents

____

____

____

____

____

____

____________________.

My grandparents laugh when

____

____

____

____

____

____

____________________.

Something special about my grandparents is

____

____

____

____

___________________.

Sometimes my grandparents

____

____

____

____

____

____

____

______________________.

My favorite thing about my grandparents is

____

____

____

____

____

_____________________.

I hope that someday my grandparents

____

____

____

____

____

____

_____________________.

I love my grandparents because

____

____

____

____

____

____

_____________________.

www.ingramcontent.com/pod-product-compliance
Lightning Source LLC
LaVergne TN
LVHW010108110826
845155LV00028B/548